Lovingly - your Daughter -

Mary

I AM

SPIRIT

The ABC's of an Ideal Spirit

MARY M RENSBERRY
JUNAI MEIJER

For information contact:

QuickTurtle Books LLC

330 Schmid Rd

Fairview, Michigan 48621

http://www.quickturtlebooks.com

Follow Mary M Rensberry at: maryrensberry.wordpress.com

Follow Artist Junai Meijer at Junai Paintings & Art on Facebook

Book and Cover design by digitechnique

ISBN: 978-1-940736-21-1

10 9 8 7 6 5 4 3 2 1

*Dedicated to
Those that fight
the good fight.*

Please...

Use a dictionary for any word or symbol that you might not know or understand.

Acknowledgements

QuickTurtle Books LLC would like to acknowledge the efforts of those whose inspiration, advice and/or editing abilities contributed to the creation of this book:

Junai Meijer - Artist, Painter & Illustrator

Richard Rensberry - Editor-in-Chief

Additionally, QuickTurtle Books LLC would like to thank the many individuals, staff and friends of QuickTurtle Books LLC, too numerous to mention, whose assistance and positive postulates & thoughts helped to make this book possible.

Without these amazing spiritual beings, this endeavor would not have been possible.

8

I AM

Junai

able.

Junai

10

I AM

Junai

beautiful.

I AM

Junai

creative.

I AM

Junai

determined.

I AM

Junai

ethical.

18

I AM
free.

Junai

20

yunai

I AM

Junai

gracious.

I AM

Junai

happy.

24

I AM

Junai

interested.

26

junai

I AM

Junai

joyful.

28

I AM

Junai

kind.

I AM

love.

I AM

Junai

myself.

junaí

I AM

Junai

natural.

I AM.

Junai

observant.

38

I AM

Junai

powerful.

junai

I AM

quick.

I AM

Junai

resolute.

44

Junai

I AM

Junai

spirit.

Yunaí

I AM

tolerant.

I AM

unique.

I AM

Junai

vital.

52

yunai

I AM

willing.

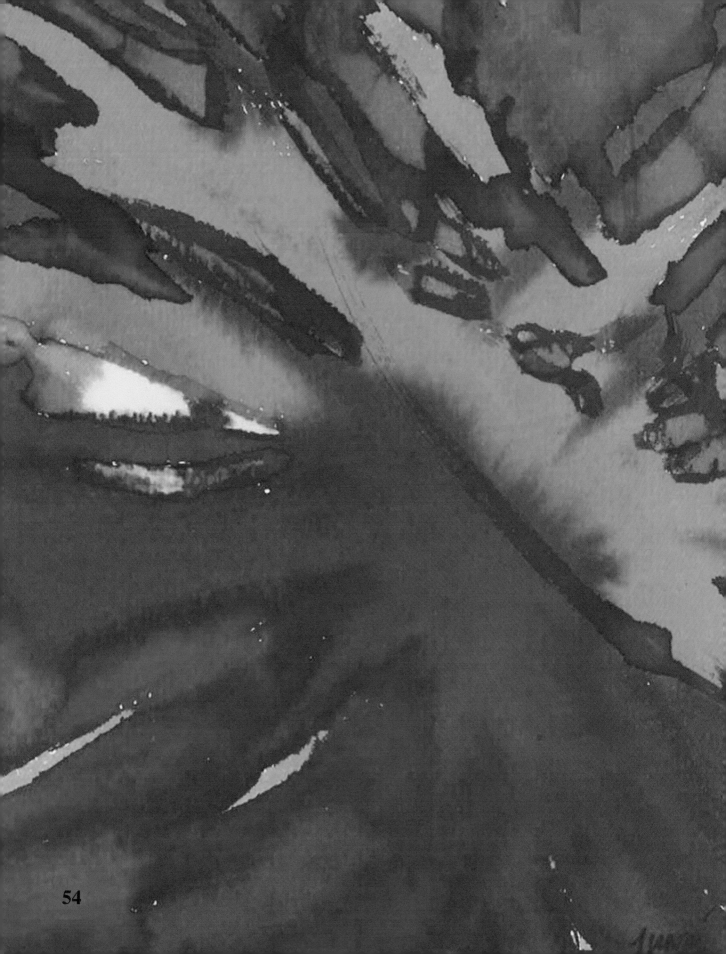

I AM

Junai

eXuberant.

I AM

Junai

youthful.

58

I AM

Junai

zealous.

I AM Spirit. I AM Spirit. I AM.... I AM Spirit. I AM Spirit. I AM Spirit.

Love Without End